CRIES

POEMS BY
IRENE E. THOMAS

© Irene E. Thomas

First Published in May 1994

All right reserved

ISBN 0 948698 08 X

British Library Cataloguing in Publication Data.
A catalogue record of this book is available from the British Library.

Published in the U.K. by
Kerin Publishers
Beech House, 29 Glan yr Afon,
Ebbw Vale, Gwent NP3 5NR

Published with the Financial Support of
The Welsh Arts Council

Made and printed in the U.K.
by J.R. Davies (Printers) Ltd.
Old Bakehouse, Church Street,
Abertillery, Gwent NP3 1EA
Tel: 0495 212600   Fax: 0495 216222

This book is sold subject to the condition that it shall not,
by any way of trade or otherwise be lent, resold, hired out,
or otherwise circulated without the publisher's prior consent
in any form of binding or cover other than that in which
it is published and without a similar condition, including this
condition, being imposed upon the subsequent purchaser.
No part of this publication may be reproduced, stored in a
retrieval system, or transmitted in any form or by any means
electronic, mechanical, photographic, recording or otherwise,
without prior permission of the authors and/or publishers.

Contents

	Page		Page
Cries	5	Singer	46
The Gulf	7	Mondays	47
Japanese Knotweed	8	Dancing on the Patch	48
Fred Ludlow's War	9	Egyptian Furnace	50
Raw Recruit	10	Dowlais Top	52
Man of Wood	11	Clydach Ironworks	53
Family Tree	12	Manmoel	54
The Row	13	Gates at Chirk	55
Writing on the Wall	16	To Ruth - Art Student	56
Any Body In	18	Ashes	57
Stained Glass	20	Welsh Doll	58
Embroidery Exhibition	21	Shadows	60
Gloves	22	Last Day at Marine Colliery	61
Dandelion Time	24	Crying the Rain	63
Poppies on Gantre	25	Dead Horse	65
Black Lead	26	Viewing Platform	66
Picking	28	Stars at the Festival	67
Coal Dust Grey	30	The Old Story	68
Sacrificial Lambs	32	Carousel	70
Davies Dago	34	Festival Sweaters	72
Rolling Pin	36	Young Valley	73
Christmas Goose	38	Gardens	74
Asking Who?	40	Fossilised	75
Moon in a Lucky Bag	41	Cages	76
Acting Grandmother	42	Autumn	78
Auntie May	43	Crying China Man	79
Tea Set	44	Epitaph	80
Telling the Runes	45		

Dedication
To my husband Keith for his support,
encouragement and enduring patience.

Acknowledgements
Cover Illustration from 'Cries of London'
by Andrew W. Tuer, published by Field and Tuer,
Leadenhall Press, 1885.

Illustrations by the Author

Cries

She sang and pounded my back.
'Hush, Hush, here comes the bogey man,
he's after little children, he'll catch them if he can.'
I wailed at the violence of the rhymes,
Jack with his bruised head and the Chipper-Chopper
cutting off last men's heads.

I resisted her terrorist activity
and kicked out at the restriction, the rough flannel binding.
She willed me to slide on a wet rubber dummy
into a sugar-dipped nightmare,
where a Sandman threw grit in burning eyes.

Changing her tune,
she soothed in her Essex dialect
with remembered Cries.
There were 'Cherries round and sound,
five pence a pound,' and,
'Tiddy Diddy dol lol.
Tiddy diddy dumplings, O.'
'Trotters'n Tripe' and 'Okey Pokey penny ice'.
I was safely wrapped in a cooney skin
with 'three rows of penny pins,
short, white and middlings.'

Now I cannot rest
or close my eyes to the crying shame,
or my ears to the death rattle of collecting boxes.
Biafra, Somalia, Save the children,
'one a penny, two a penny.'

'Buy a lucky card for leukaemia,
a raffle ticket for a kidney machine,
a green broom to sweep away pollution.'

'Buy my sweet Ecstasy.'

There are still knives to grind
and bombs do not discriminate.

At Bishopsgate,
medieval glass shattered
into cutting edges,
'Chipper Chopper'

Marks or Harrods,
the scare is the same,
and the cries.

The Gulf

In Market Street,
the bloodshot eye of the butcher's
glared over the cold-to-perishing Crossing,
where Hughes, Gospel Hall, paraded,
sandwiched between the Blood of The Lamb
and the Day of Judgement.
After an explosion of oratory,
his evangelical breath hung like gunsmoke
over housewives, right dressing,
shouldering bags and giving orders,
while they chewed over economical cuts
and fall-out lamb.

Hoisted on steel hooks,
the common herd of carcasses
flanked one side of the shop.
The voice invaded.

'And the word was made flesh and dwelt among us.'

Frozen bodies swayed gently in acquiescence,
but there were no ears to hear.

'That Saddam is a real butcher
and all those poor birds covered in oil.'
'I want a nice chicken.
One that doesn't look dead when it's cooked.'
'Sorry, only pieces left,
legs, breasts and wings.'

Steel grated on cutting edges,
a neck was hacked with a chopper,
bones splintered.

'That enough?'

Japanese Knotweed

This oriental was part of my childhood,
although I did not then know its name,
or that we would be at war.

It filled the next door garden
where bouncing rubber balls
were captured in a curtain of bamboo.
We watched them rot
and could not reach out or rescue.

We cut blow-pipes from its hollow stems
and dried peas hurtled on our breath
to sting the arms of unsuspecting Mams,
hanging Persil Whites.
With lethal darts we wounded seedy Germans,
dropping in parachutes of thistle-down,
over Gantre.

From this Knotweed we carved penny whistles,
to play the tune the donkey died on
and its lightweight stems framed home-made kites.
We pasted the sky
with flour and water and Co-op brown paper.

It was left in peace until the intrusion,
and then the hold became too strong for riddance
and it would not yield to steel or blade,
but ran underground and shot up
with blood-tipped shoots upon our common ground.

The silent invader has dug-in,
spread Triffid-like over spaces
and there are plans for mass destruction.

Fred Ludlow's War

After standing for King and Country,
an invasion of picture-goers
from the Palace and the White House
charged into the perishing night
and down the hill to Fred's,
where the smell of frying chips
spread a warm blessing, between Libanus and the Prims.

Ammunition ready, Fred served in his striped shirt,
his bald head shining like the domed covers of his pans.

Tails and cutlets, coated with flour and water
dropped delicately from his nicotined fingers,
floated in boiling oil until the skin blistered.

'Mrs' Ludlow, the evacuee,
doled out Cockney with the Cod and the crackling
and hair-raising stories of the Blitz,
her permanent, a shock around her face.
The daughter leaned provocatively over the counter
making fish-eyes at the exempt and the medically unfit,
getting an eye-full of her see-through blouse,
in spite of steam.

At first, bullies and agressors elbowed to the front
and demanded their three penny-worth.
Small-fry went to the wall.
Then we joined up and queued for equal rations,
lined the wooden counter,
where the scrubbed grain stood to attention.

Spread over news, dark stains blotted out Dunkirk.
The salty liquid soaked through
and under battering, soldiers tore.

We were too young to serve
but while we waited our turn,
we drank Fred's vinegar,
and he played war with us.

Raw Recruit

Rain polished the pewter street,
outside the Citadel.
It washed away the Saturday suns
chalked on the pavement by the old soldier,
drawing dreams of Summer Lands.
His white-sailed ships,
sank in a concrete sea.

They beat the drum, and it drew me in,
out of the wet night into the Sunshine Hour.

It was light and music
brass-bright and toe-tapping.
Recruits, badged and bonnet-ed,
buttoned up and bursting,
clapping and fighting the Good Fight.
Clashing, skin-tight tambourines
on elbows and knees,
ribbons flying,
faces red with effort and the gladness of it all.

Volunteering, I climbed the steps.
The Captain held me up above the rostrum
and I sang of a bird, and how God had taught it to fly.

Still in the Light,
I ran home down the dark tunnel of the back bailey,
forgetting bogey-men,
head full of Good News and Hallelujahs.

'I'm going to join the Army, Mam.'

'You' she said, pouring cold water,
'are in the Wesleyans,
and there you'll stay!'

I had not been near the war,
but knew I was already a prisoner.

Man of Wood

They sat
still and derelict as empty houses.

He was part of the furniture,
pushed into the corner,
a crochet blanket doubled over his knees.

Someone mentioned wood
and a door opened in a dark room.

Coming through,
'I knew wood,' he said.
He blinked and leaned forward,
as if to see better into the past.
'First, I made a boat.'
He held it, cradling the hull
and ran his blunted finger over the polished deck.
'A dresser next,
out of old Wincarnis boxes,
with only a saw and a hammer.'
He brought down a steel fist, without impact
on the soft chains and twisted trebles.
'It came up like mahogany.'

He whispered its name
as though it was the Word of God.

The vacant lots listened,
but only heard echoes,
as if a shutter banged
and momentarily disturbed.

An institutional cup of tea,
thrust into his hands
washed away his concentration.
He went in again
and closed the door.

Family Tree

The line of descent is down Marine,
rooted in the galleries,
along veins hacked and mandrilled
until the black humour gushed to the surface
and traced William Street as birthplace.

There was no field-work,
and poor sustenance for young shoots.
Fungoid dole spread its mouldy pittance
over the hopes of my father
and unable to bear the weight,
this branch broke
and left us hanging on strap.

In time,
lover's hearts and initials
cut deep with a name in common
and the binding together eased the hard graft.
An age of iron and steel,
generated in the furnaces at Victoria,
made sparks fly.

On the maternal side, the tree thrived,
off-shoots reached up to stars,
and Castor and Pollux
were born with steel spoons in their mouths.

There were some golden days before the downfall,
when supports were wrenched away with family ties.

At the top of the tree
a gnarled finger
traces the empty sky.
This branch has not borne fruit.

The Row

Just risen from sleep
in its corrugated sheets and brass bedsteads,
the Row staggers along the mountain,
its unwashed face grey with yesterday's grime.

At intervals,
a tympany of tin baths hang on six inch nails,
tom-toms for small boys.

Blankets beat on lines tightly strung,
and blow in common time,
fingered by children running underneath,
sharply reprimanded.

In his garden,
Mr. Davies grows dandelions through rusty pushchairs,
                                           tyres,
                                           eggshells,
                                           a pink laced corset,
                                           ashes and old daps.

Auntie Lizzie's blue-bells
shoot from a starburst of leaves,
cobalt rockets full-stopped with geums,
orange suns in a sapphire sky.

Under a gooseberry bush, behind the coal cwch,
Elsie Hutchins and Cy. Jones make love.
There will be jam when the harvest comes,
spread on a new batch from the Co-op,
or a bun from the oven,
with too many mouths to feed.

In the dry-ash lav. of number nine,
Jakey Johnson sits
marking his coupon with indelible noughts and crosses.
In this sanctuary from his strict Baptist wife,
he prays to the Great God Littlewood,
to bless him with a cheque for £10,000.
On the wooden seat,
he flies to Las Vegas and Monte Carlo,
and spins fantasies of Roulette, Baccarat,
Strip Jack Naked and loaded dice.

'Making your will out there, are you?'
The cold water voice, flung out of the kitchen,
dashes his dreams.

Children suck the edge of the table in number eight,
eyes wide, watching her breath-sharp knife
circling sour apples,
dropping lovers names.
She wipes her hands on a pinny,
stretched tightly over her middle,
like the pastry over pregnant lumps of apple.
A kiss of sugar then,
to sweeten a satisfying tart.

Bronwen Parry, last house,
usherette at the new palatial Plaza,
looks in the fly-marked mirror
nailed over the soap dish
and pinches her finger waves, set with Amami,
the image of Ginger Rogers, or perhaps Alice Faye.

Mr. Jenkins
sits and fights for breath.
With failing strength hammers segs into shoes,
wishing he could patch his leather lungs.

On the corner, gangs of kids wait
for Maggie to come home from the Club.
They circle
and she picks up her frayed black skirts
until her pink bloomers show,
and dances.

Writing On the Wall

The stones were curved and rhubarb red
on the top of the wall,
where we sat and dangled our legs
over hearses ringed with wreaths
and counted a rash of mourners
in black-head bowlers,
dark ties and Sunday trousers.

We sat astride the stones,
riding stallions into sunsets,
sailing the Queen Mary
and driving to Barry Island in our own cars.

With slivers of slate,
we scratched lovers names,
and sent arrows through broken hearts.
'Wyndham loves Violet',
'Dereck loves Violet',
'Violet loves Mervyn Price'.

Played games with noughts and crosses,
wrote slogans
'VOTE
VOTE
VOTE
FOR 'NEURIN BEVAN'.

Made drawings of Maggie Davies,
fag stuck to her lip,
Patty Mason, head white with nits,
Shirley Temple
and Billy Prosser with his small glass eye.

We chalked
nick-names and rude names.
Olwen Parry was dirty.

Wrote 'KNICKERS'
and drew a man without clothes.
Two dots for eyes,
one for his belly button.
Sun's shining through pit wheel spokes,
children with crooked legs,
stick men and women with holes for eyes,
birds flying.
Houses in Rows
with windows in corners,
chimney with scribble for smoke,
clouds on horizons,
paths leading no-where.

Any Body In

On my own,
looking for the King,
I turned the iron ring of St. Johns,
and the door cleared the chessboard,
checking His porch.

I hecked over on whites
and looked down the polished aisle,
a slippery path for changelings,
who cursed, and flew kites on Bufton's,
but after sacraments of surplice and lace,
and mouths washed out with Fairy,
transformed to Sunday Saints.

I sat in the sacred pews
of Mr. Parry, Warden and Mr. Jones, Confirmed,
where they had a better view of God,
and looked up to where He kept his place,
behind the curtain at the altar.
I remembered to curtsy,
like Vicar Davies, unable to rise,
his silver buckled shoe,
caught in the hem of his garment.

Crossing the Jordan of the blue carpet
to His table, laid for supper,
I took comfort in the material of the cloth,
edged with Martha Morgan's crochet,
created in her Colliers' Row kitchen,
where she sat,
making holes in hours with her hook,
with ashes to raise
and unwashed dishes wedged in her concrete bosh.

I blessed the earthy presence of Mrs. Solway,
Newtown, Seventh Row back,
all elbow-grease and cross-over pinny,
brasso-ing the wings of the eagle
and spitting on her rag
to cat-lick the face of the angel.

My tongue dry as salt, I drew back the curtain,
and unbelieving,
put out my hand to touch cold grey stone.
There was no vision.

I looked at the furnishings,
the empty chairs,
an unopened Bible on the throw-over cloth,
the candlesticks and ornamental vases.

It was His front room,
for weddings, funerals and Sundays.
God was no different from us.
<u>We</u> lived out the back
and kept the front for show.

In the porch,
the vicar came, calling, playing his own game,
making moves from black to Bishop.

I ran down the aisle to save him.
'There's nobody in,' I said.

Stained Glass

As fragile as a May-fly's wing,
yet weathering the winds of heaven.

River sand and beechwood ash,
fused by fire and stained,
an ancient art of alchemy, secrets kept.

In church and chancel, cloister and cathedral,
glaziers laboured with grozers and shears,
stopping knives and lathekins.
They hammered fire into stone,
giving a greater vision
of saints in true colours.
Passed through flame,
their auras glow with spiritual fire,
ruby, amber and amethyst.
Fish netted into cobalt seas,
waves stilled with calms.
Bird, leaf and butterfly,
intensify in inner darkness.

Base metal comes between pieces of God,
and fragments of angels,
in the Eye of the Dean at Lincoln.
Shaped in a different setting,
Adam and Eve walk with leaden feet,
away from a rose-coloured garden.
Flaws and grits, made in human error,
have value as a means to light.

Man can look at moon and see himself,
but in that moment when illumination comes,
the light of Spirit is too bright.

Yet between the blindness and the vision,
there is a screen, a filtering,
and looking up, through tinted glass,
he sees the ultimate design.

Embroidery Exhibition
Hereford Cathedral

Broiderers see God through the eye of a needle,
weave fine thread over chancel walls,
Chinese silk, peacock lamé, damask and cloth of gold,
are gathered on the fabric of this ancient place,
where cloth and stone have equal weight.

Embroideries, flat as Mappa Mundi,
catch light from glass, stained and beaded.
Sequins and mylar and twisted purls,
burn in Pentecostal blazes.

They furnished the House of the Lord
with kneelers spiked with thorns.

A Mothers Union banner,
corded and couched in wild silk and laidwork,
hangs heavy with Virgin and Child.
A white dove, whipped and chained,
flies into a chiffon sun.

St. Clement, caught with herring bone,
is anchored with sail-cloth and sacking,
drowning in a stranded sea,
with images of saints, stabbed and split-stitched.

In a weaker design,
seven satin apostles stagger in wine and port
and on coarser ground, a canvas cock crows.

Braided and latticed with silver,
some pieces are for sale,
other hangings could not be bought.

Threadbare,
I once worshipped in patches and stitches
and saw angels.
Among this material,
there were none.

Gloves

Made for a Queen, in pale buff leather,
fine fingers unsoiled.
Noblemen and satin-backed horses,
career around the gauntlet,
between floss-silk flowers and seedings.

In cruder cut, a working glove,
its hardened skin,
a natural protection from cuffs,
fingers etched in whorls,
imprinted under water
with caustic soda and aching Blue.

And in my skin-tight flesh,
I hold together, all thumbs,
a fingerless mitten,
frayed on outer edges.
Seams come apart,
but at best, in this doe-skin,
it is a means to grasp the sting and the thorn.

When the right one is lost
the other, unprotected, feels the burn.

One left,
a transparent network on a stretcher.

When the crumbling finger
slides into its final glove of wood,
it touches fire
and writes its epitaph in rising smoke.

English, early
17th

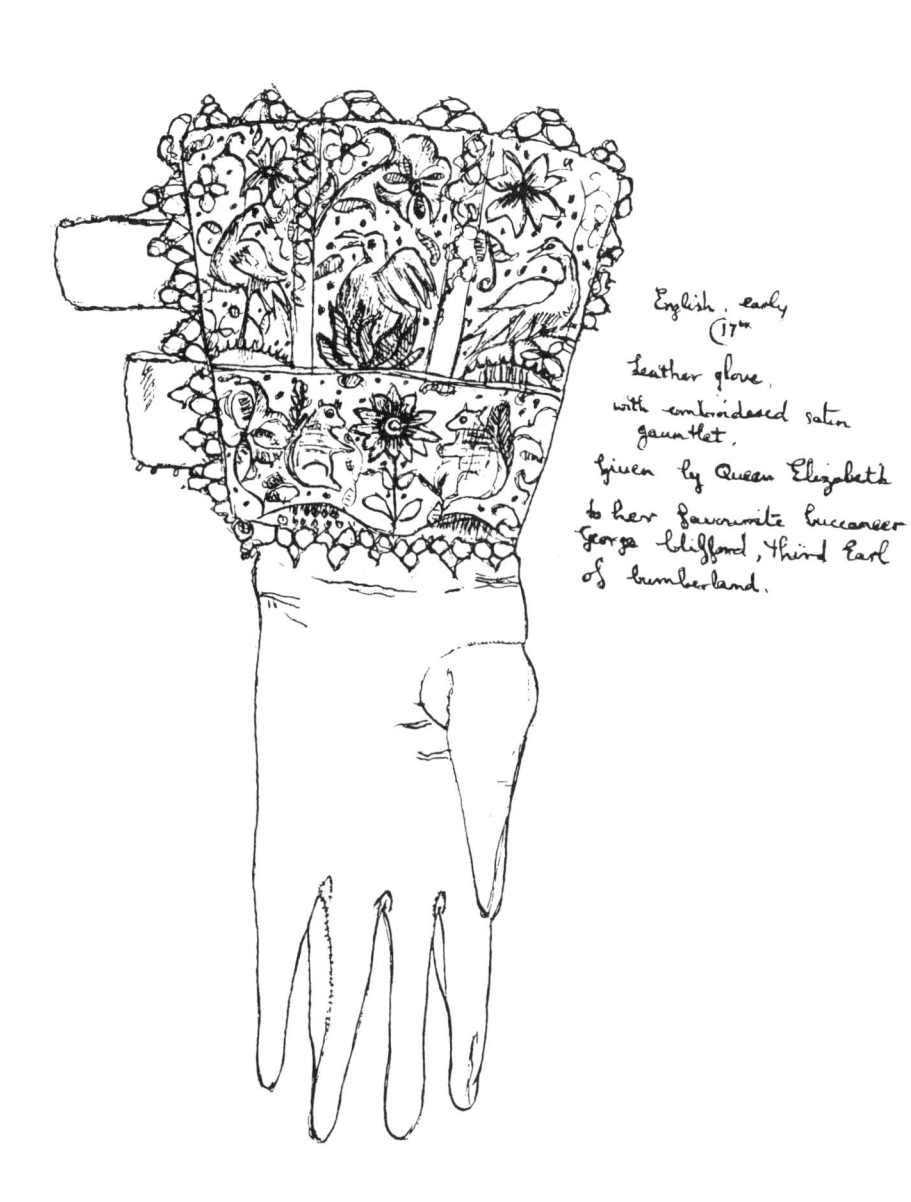

Leather glove,
with embroidered satin
gauntlet,

given by Queen Elizabeth
to her favourite buccaneer
George Clifford, Third Earl
of Cumberland.

Dandelion Time

We bunched the milky hollows of their stems
and thrust them into rusty cans
to decorate half brick houses
cemented with muck and gobs of imagination.
Pee-the-beds, pulled from overlays of shale,
were stirred in stews of lazy daisies
in a cack-handed pan.

When their sun had changed to moon,
we blew on them to tell the time,
one o'clock, two o'clock, three o'clock, four,
not counting days or measuring hours.
They spiralled from our fingers
to circle wind in summer snow.
They rode on flanks of ponies, until out of puff,
flocked old Sammy's beard
and the ticking on his mattress
where he slept, come opening time.

On the tip edge,
Wyndham Parry,
tired of asking daisies,
blew down soft kisses
to his love in Colliers Row.

Poppies on Gantre

Outcasts,
thrown clear of the confines of a wedlock of wire,
sewing wild seed in dry ash,
grew rampant as docks and dandelions.

They felt the drumming of the valley wind,
burst through brittle shale
and in the carnival of the morning
paraded, striped and black busby'd
brash as young jazz bands.

We looked to them for entertainment
and in their orange amphitheatres
watched bees perform their pollen dances.

Buds, easy in embryonic sleep,
nodded and swayed to music half-remembered,
but we ripped their green bellies
with sharp-edged nails,
underlined with Gantre grime.
Hooked out folded frills and un-ironed skirts,
made them dance to our beating
until they dropped
and left them gutted,
purple and pink,
barren on Gantre.

Black-Lead

Boot brushes,
one for shining, one for spit.
Survivors from the polish box
behind the pantry door,
where they rubbed shoulders
with dusters,
tins of Brasso,
Zebra,
Nugget,
and Rising Sun for the stove.

Bristles stiff with blacking,
interlocked and clung together,
as we did on darker days
when there was black-lead in our hearts
as well as on our boots.

It was all blacking,
every day of our Cherry-Blossomed, boot-licking lives.

Bar-shoes and brogues
with laces crossed for luck,
irons, door stops and fenders.
Polishing fire bricks and slates into mirrors,
dark enough to ask who was the fairest.
Even wished we could polish the night
to reflect in the Ty Bach.

We climbed the garden path
and in our cupped hands, the tallow flame died.
The night edged round in memorial,
black as the stinking stumbling back alley
and the twelve-o-clock front road,
running dark as senna,
after mean-fisted street lights dowted.

We slept under an icy pitch of slates,
in bedrooms, black as tar.

In the cold knee-cracking morning,
acrid-black lead smeared our breath
filled the kitchen like sal-volatile,
but ashes risen,
we knew the satisfaction of burnished brass
and clean boots on the top step,
their polished-apple toes
ready to kick the day.

Picking

When there was no more school
and the sun had been out for two weeks,
it was time for picking.

Whinberries covered Mynydd Carn-y-Cefn,
ankle deep and untrodden,
as the carpet in Auntie Beat's front room.

We climbed the mountain road
under Morning Star,
carrying jam jars,
throttled with string handles.

Gran sat like a queen under her beehive hat
minding the jars,
while workers brought her berries to pick over.
Her long skirt reeved,
and we saw her thin legs
ringed in black wool stockings.

The steamy finger of the long feeder below,
pointed rudely to the stripping
and rolling into sheets.
Concrete coolers
blew off acrid fumes into wind,
turning to smuts, on wagging tongues.

We sat in the Gods
with the navy-blue nobs in the jars,
fingers touched with royal purple,
teeth blackened, and on edge against the grit.

Above it all,
where the skylark sang its vertical song
and pale moths disturbed from sleep
in White Ladies Bedstraw,
fluttered to leaves,
burned by the gawping sun.

We trailed home,
to hot whimberry tart from the side oven,
crisp, sugared and set in skin-tight custard.
Back to clinker and ash, to pick a harder fruit.

Coal Dust Grey
(Colliers Row 1930)

Washing
billowing across the bailey,
shirts and spencers,
combinations,
merging into
coal dust grey.

Turn the mangle,
pound the dolly.
Wooden pegs dance on the line,
sheets and blankets
turned to middle,
patched and washed
a coal dust grey.

Baby clothes,
their pristine whiteness
hanging short
on rusty lines,
cradled in the grimy breezes,
growing into
coal dust grey.

'Quick it's raining',
grab the washing,
joust the prop, wind in the line.
Make your Mam
a living clothes horse,
saddled
with the coal dust grey.

Pit and mangle, move together,
married in an endless motion.
Starch and blue-bag,
pick and shovel,
turning love
a coal dust grey.

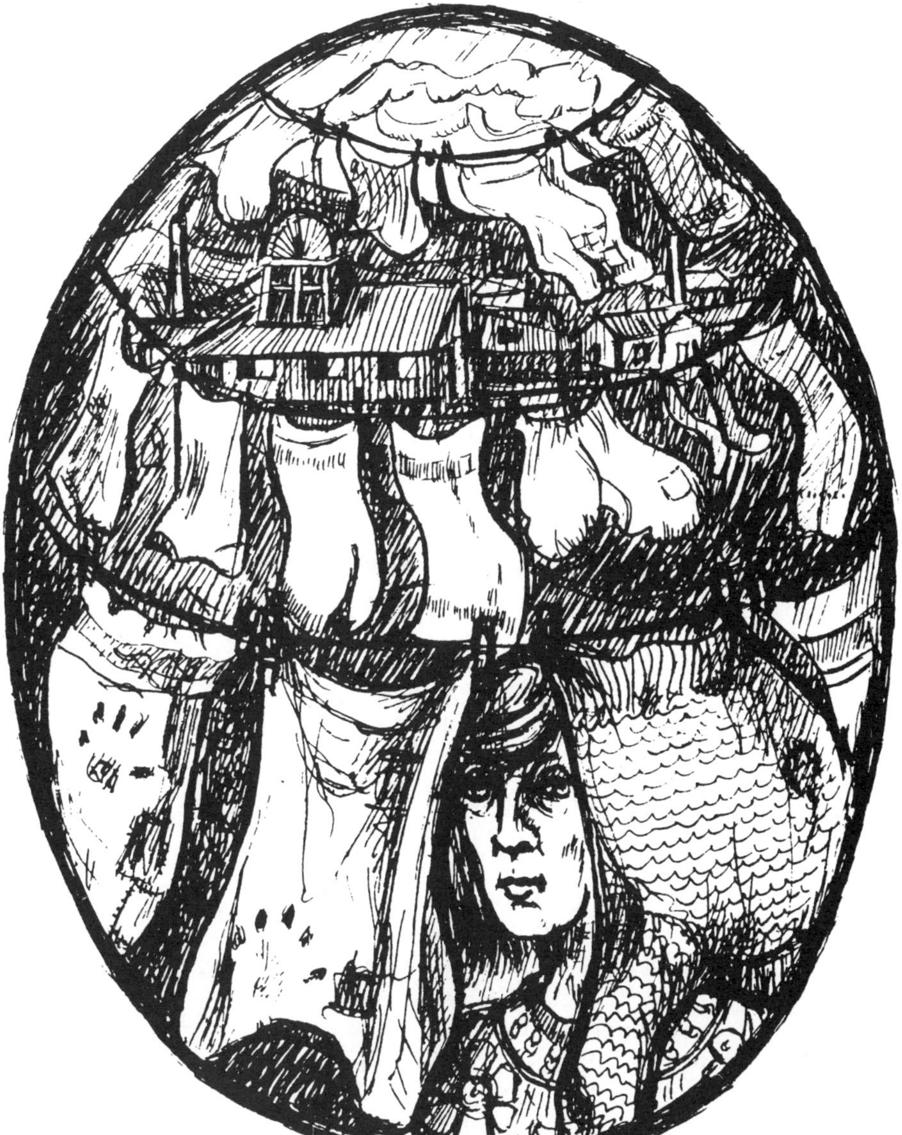

Sacrificial Lambs

I first heard the black ones crying
and learned of their fleecing
as I wet-breathed
through the warmth of their fibres.

They cropped the tip
until cold snaps worried,
and they foraged in Colliers Row,
pawing buckets until they spilled,
grazing ice with clinker and ash.

In the night came the crack of horn on wood
as they rammed shored-up gates,
and shouldered into frozen gardens,
gnawing at stunted stalks and sprouts
solid as a sinker's knuckles.

They sheltered in gulleys between the houses,
and dry-coughed the darkness away.

Stiff and ravenous,
they matted outside half doors,
heading for curled peelings and outside leaves.

In spite of meagre staple,
came lambs, born on Gantre shale,
and we heard them bleating
for lost mothers and for milk,
and there was no shepherd,
except for the counting and the killing.

In summer,
ewes panted under patchy winter coats,
scrubbed skin raw
and left woollen shreds
hanging on black tar wires.

The old ones
defended against dogs who threatened
and losers made carrion for crows.
Jack-daws,
loud mouthed keepers of the pecking order,
spread a shivering pall, bruise-black
over common branding and seared flesh.

A few grey hairs remained,
and a scattering of teeth
worn down with grinding.

They were poor man's meat
and on the chopping block
their heads split
with tempered blade and pounder,
half-brained with steel.
Tongues stilled in aspic.

Davies Dago

A toff from Swansea,
he slept in a kiln, shared with mountain sheep.

They accepted the common smell of his ankle-length coat,
and the familiar fragrance of dried-out lavender,
he had gathered from front gardens,
where wire fences tarred and teased their wool.
The sound of his barking cough
did not worry or send them running.

Turfed out at half-past-seven of a morning
by Arthur Blaenavon and Sweeney Todd,
labourers at Beaufort Brickworks,
he ate like a gentleman, from a billy-can
bright as the windows of Siloam in the sun,
clean as the surface of the Boat Pond,
scoured by East wind.

As he chewed his hard cheese,
he watched workers cutting, sorting and mixing clay
gouged from spoil heaps on Llangynidr.
Saw them sweat, setting bricks in ovens,
leaving finger room between.
Women in canvas aprons, laced-up shoes and tams,
stacked and wheeled, barrows swaying,
round pillar caps and plinths,
beaded jambs and chamfered copings.

Ramming his slouch hat over his eyes,
he gathered his Almanacks and darning needles,
sold to housewives, patching and mooning.
Remembered the sprats Mrs. Evans cooked of a Friday dinner,
and the little hobble he had promised to do for Mrs. Price,
liberal with her apple tart, after prophecies from Old Moore.

Well oiled, with a few glasses of her elderberry,
and a half of cider, bought for a penny halfpenny
at the Globe Inn on the Rise,
he went to sleep in a warm bed,
bundled in a fleecy blanket.

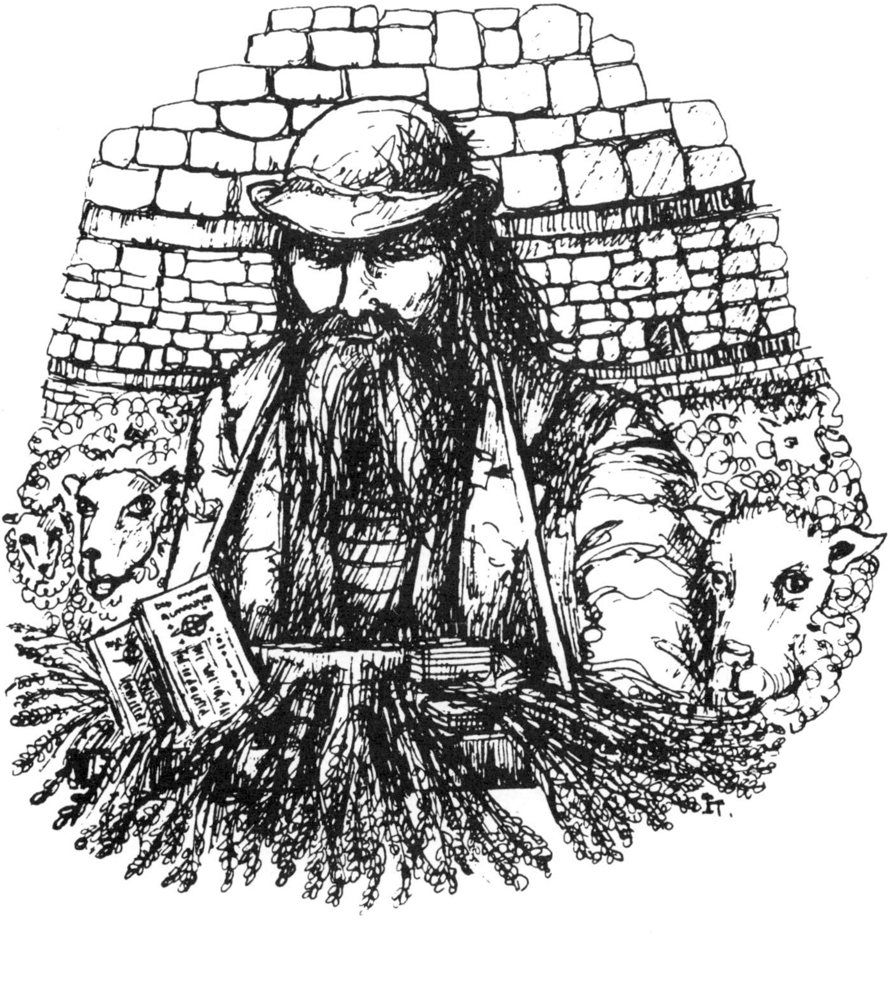

Rolling Pin

It is the colour of warm gingerbread,
an old tool, oiled with suet and loose lard,
scorch-marked from the griddle and the baking.

Eyes level with the edge of the table,
I watched its easy wooden handles
rotate under her fists,
four bone moons, pushing an ocean of pastry,
making waves which fanned out
into a spume of Self-Raising.
She hoisted pastry on to the pin like a snail,
and dredging,
slapped it down full bellied on the board.

She rolled to even thickness,
and when it lay flat as spilled milk,
she stamped out rounds with serrated edges,
and laid them over black holes of patty tins,
indented with stars and shells.
I saw the soft white circles
sag under the weight of Golliwog Raspberry,
delicately scraped off a tea spoon
with her little finger.

Rolling up,
she tented over chunks of cooking apple,
and sometimes over wild bramble and whinberry.
Her hand spread beneath the enamel plate,
and she spun it on the edge of a knife,
cutting a perfect ring,
then forked a frill around the edges, to tart.

The pin was never washed,
'makes it stick,' she said,
and coaxed it clean with a damp cloth and a dusting,
then hung it from its string, stiff with flour
on its own six inch nail in the pantry.

Sometimes, she used it as a weapon,
always promising,
especially to my Grandfather,
home late from the Con. Club,
stumbling against the front room furniture in the dark.
His shame-face glowed
through the half opened middle door,
and with a mumbled 'Go' night Em',
he disappeared into the back bedroom,
without his supper of tongue pie.

Now, when I reach for her belaying pin,
with an urge to flatten,
I remember how she spared the rod, and smoothed over,
with a cool hand and a light touch.

Christmas Goose

Downstairs,
I had heard of the Gander and the violence.

I watched the annual pantomime of goose feathers,
the hissing and the cackling.

My Grandmother,
knee-deep in down,
plucked the Christmas goose.
Feathers flew from her fingers
and cushioned the wooden chairs,
settled a white cover on the table.

I clapped my hands
and the feathers danced to set patterns
over the oiled cloth,
a ballet along familiar lines.

They hung in the air
and with a sharp intake,
filled my mouth until I spat out.

I stuffed armfulls into bolsters
and pillows cased in ticking.
Up to my elbows in warm snow,
I chilled.

The pimples
and the comic appearance of the stripped bird
gave rise to old chestnuts.

'His goose is cooked',
drew ribald laughter-come-to-crying.

Upstairs, on chesty nights,
I slipped into goose-greased dreams,
held between the bony knees of nightmare.

White winged sheets beat like angels guarding,
as my grandfather played his part
with the cutting edge,
and circled the long white neck
of Mother Goose with a gash of ruby.

I buried my face in the pillow
to deaden the screaming and the song,
but feathers suffocated.

Asking 'Who'?

On the three times-a-day Sabbath,
we took our spiritual medicine,
and after the glory and the after-meeting,
when Ezra always thanked God
for showers of blessings
and only asked for 'droppings',
the door closed on our Halleujahs
and we faced the night.
It pressed its fingers against our eye-balls
to ask us 'Who'?
but those who had seen the light,
said the Name.

We prayed for the hell-fire doors down below
to open and lighten our darkness
and then we walked in flames like Shadrach.

There were no angels,
only out-of-the-body wraiths from coolers
belching white clouds into the steamy dark.
They wreathed the empty chapel,
silent as a headstone.

Other spectres haunted,
silver and steel hanging overhead.
Locos screamed at partings,
and trucks shouldered each other
and we heard the dull thud of dead weight.

We picked our way past shored-up houses,
cracking like cannons in the night
and shivering, clung together,
uncertain of our footing
and tried to remember the warmth of the hymns
and the word of God
which told us not to be afraid.

Moon in a Lucky Bag

In Fairy tales
they say that when you know
the name of a spirit,
power is diminished,
the hold is weakened
and the fear.

We waited for his coming
as if he were Messiah.
At the appointed time between two and five,
he appeared at the Bargoed Emporium.
It was all jingle, coloured lights
and dreams wrapped in paper parcels.
A Tooth Fairy
who could fill an aching gap with silver,
waved her wand over the coinage
and sent it to Toyland on overhead wires.

I sat in his red lap,
harder than I had imagined,
in an aura of humbug and told him my name.
He asked for a kiss
and promised me the moon in a lucky bag.

When they told me,
I cried in disbelief,
then I recalled the dish-pan hands of the fairy,
his bony knees and the peppermint breath.

I had often seen him
slumped on a seat in the Old Man's Park,
disguised in a Dai-cap and long greasy mac,
watching children swinging on the Witches Hat,
and offering his hot breath sweets.

Acting Grandmother

She never drew back the curtain,
only half-appeared
in the spotlight of my searching questions.

Once, she let me reach out
and curl my fingers round her hand-span waist.
She was hard and rigid as a Russian doll,
her peasant costume, a sacking apron
splayed over a skirt in black-out rep.

I marvelled at her magic,
conjuring quilts from patches and scraps,
and crochet lace from invisible thread.
She changed dandelion and nettle to wine,
bottling up a sunburst on the tongue,
a sting around the edges.

Without prompting,
she never dried on Catechism, Psalm or Creed,
and sometimes chanted old Music Hall songs,
rhythmic, but tuneless,
and almost came through, remembering stars.

I often watched the nightly performance
as she high-stepped out of her petticoats,
then turning, gathered up the flannel bouquet
of Wintergreen and Fiery Jack.

Holding in,
she unhooked her stays, shored with whalebone,
and keeping to routine, loosened her puckered shimmy.
It was lined with Thermogene, tacked in each winter
and worn until Hawthorn was out.

Under cover,
she threw up her arms in a final gesture
and the wincyette gown she slept in
wreathed around her bowed shoulders.

I missed her, when the curtains closed.

Auntie May

Looking up, I searched for her on Saturdays,
a speck on the shoulder of Mynydd Carn y Cefn,
sweeping down the hill
between Sixth and Seventh Rows,
and across the valley to our kitchen,
which she filled with laughter-come-to-crying.

Smart as the catalogue ladies I cut out for fun,
she queened it in coloured beads and real diamanté.
I listened, all pigs ears,
while she poured out a stream of jokes with her tea,
and chewed on stories about budgies,
God, and her neighbours in Limestone Road.
My six year-old sides split and I had stitches.

Come Christmas, she gave me a 'whoopee' cushion
and a six-inch nail labelled, 'coat hanger'.
Filled a black woollen stocking for Gran
with coal, a packet of lard
and a square of Recketts Blue from the pantry.
Every Year Gran was surprised.

Auntie May came to my wedding,
in a jumble sale hat
perked with a spray of Woolworth's feathers,
squirming round a stalk.
Stuck in at an awkward angle,
they made me feel uncomfortable.

Lipstick ran into cracks around her mouth
and laughter lines dried in a parched pink foundation.
Her mauve chiffon scarf, tied in a kittenish bow,
clashed with loud yellow of her cardigan.
The gaudy beads rattled.

She pulled at my clothes,
wanting to tell me the same old jokes.
I smiled politely.

Tea Set

Our common cups
were all odds and nothing matched.
It was rag-and-bone china
exchanged for a bag of hand-me-downs.
The thick-lipped earthenware pieces,
had cracks in the glazing
which showed up the poverty of the material.
We drank our tea down to dregs
which afterwards damped down the small.

Our best set was put by,
wrapped carefully in 'The Chronicle'
and only brought out for visitors.
This superior set,
with side dishes wreathed in rose-buds,
was laid out on a dead-white cloth,
rigid with Robin Starch.
When Uncle Jack came to tea,
he spoke Cardiff posh
and puffed out from his pipe
a blessing in a cloud of Balkan Sobrani.

He stirred a sharp-tongued slice of lemon
into his beverage
and we managed wry smiles.

It was polite bread and butter first,
and no mucking in to the boughten sponge,
no burping or slurping
and we drank
with little fingers up in the world.

Telling The Runes

She regularly doled out a serving of six.
Swallowing hard,
I sucked the black swollen skins
and laid out hard cores
on the curved edge of the dish.
Gran told the runes,
but the prophecy was always the same,
one too many came to 'Poor Man'.

More pinch and scrape, turning the knife in pots
over barren seeds of raspberry
or smears of salmon and shrimp.
This glass was not clear,
but still we cast about for fortune
in sand, tea and Devil's cards.
Looked for diamonds in dregs
and a dark man with a ring of gold.

We had no need of Tinker or Tailor,
did our own mending and cutting out.
The solitary iron bee in its wooden hive,
hummed every evening,
and Gran kept time on the treadle with her foot,
while it's steel tongue licked shimmies into shape.

We counted soldiers. Albert next door,
with blanco-ed belt and spit and polish boots,
khaki rough as his tongue,
and Ivor, whose Navy collar we touched for luck,
but there was no future in it.

It never came to Beggar, that was too much.
'Feed your own' Gran maintained.

Hoping to take avoiding action,
I only ate five.

It did not work.

Singer

The silver tongue was mute under the polished cover
but when it saw daylight
its song filled the dark corners of my childhood.

Golden scrolls feathered the sleek black body,
and its breast puffed out at the extravagance of the design.
This deep-throated songster
moved to the rhythms of my grandmother's slippered foot,
dipping and rising on the iron lace of the treadle
and keeping time with her tuneless hum
of troubles packed up and how her heart was in Tipperary.
It was hard going when the tension grew too great
and the thread snapped, but she fed it through thick and thin
over sackcloth and white sheets turned to middle.

Nesting in its magpie drawer,
a collection of spindles and shuttles,
darners and pitted thimbles, a Newey Wizard bodkin,
and a linen tape to measure growing pains.
Pins in pink paper,
a gift from the Emporium instead of farthing change,
an amber bead and an army button dying for Brasso.

When its voice grew hoarse, it was well-oiled
and glided over binders, christening gowns
and Whitsun fine feathers.
Its foot hopped over seams and joins
as I did over cracked paving.
It was silent as war was declared,
but this bird-in-hand was brought into service,
made-do and mended, blind-stitched over blackout,
and flew over parachute silk,
a cold skin clinging to a body.

When the beating was finished, it was out of action
and laid in the glory hole.

Afterwards, it was sold for a song.

Mondays

On washdays, I was underfoot,

After the soft-soaping,
sheets wound over her arms,
snaked around her neck,
twisting
as she wrung out.

I lost her in suds and steam.

Tugging at strings,
they puckered up,
sucking wet kisses and clung to each other,
then pulled away with a smack.
They touched her gently
as she set the prop against the line
like an arrow.

'I love' she said
'to see them blow on a good day.'

When they were dry,
she filled her arms,
warmed,
smoothed,
tucked them in.

Afterwards, she was too tired.

Dancing on the Patch
Blackwood 1938

We sat on the right side of Libanus,
cherubic in stiff-necked Sunday Best,
trying not to fidget
and put straight-laced boots
into the back of the pay-down pews.
The preacher poured sweat into praises
and haloes slipped as we bent our heads
playing eye-ball with secret abstainers,
who had not closed their lids
or put their hands together.

The windy sermon
milled around our ears in double-Dutch
and we hot-handed sweets behind our backs
until we were Palm-toffee-jawed,
with butter unmelted.

In the after meeting,
the congregation asked for blessing
and we prayed
for the benediction of the summer evening,
longing to race home
and change to other glad-rags,
leavened with a peck of dirt.

In Garfield Street,
they wheeled out the piano
and the tight-lipped shalt-nots
closed their windows and clicked their tongues,
while the sermon tasters
unbuckled their front-room Bibles,
and chewed over.

We danced on the Patch to the music,
in company with neighbours,
squiffy clubbies and sparkers,
and sent the Sunday angels packing.

Devilment unleashed,
we danced widdershins in abandoned whirls,
swearing like the hellers we were,
and all the Puritan in the world
could not wash out our mouths.

Egyptian Furnace
Rhymney Valley - 1989

At Abertysswg, boys swing on the one tree,
a hanging rope, and kick against the empty sky.

Houses turn their bare backs to the sharp November sun
and point out scraped hills,
pierced and tunnelled and gutted for coal.

In Rhymney, leaves burn without warmth
and in this catch-cold valley,
there is no furnace to warm the pocket,
only the self-important slag is busy,
elbowing through reclamation grass.

It was once the Valley of the Kings,
the Ironmasters, their conical pyramids,
black memorials to the great Gods of Iron and Steel.

The Egyptian Furnace at Bute,
built like the Temple at Dendera,
enslaved workers who paid homage to the Company Shop.
with a promise of food and clothing in the life to come.
High Priests performed last rites as fire died.

Spirit departed, chapels wrap their outside skins
around mummified rostrums and mouldering hymnals.
They ache to fall down
and rest their stiff-backed, pay-down pews
among sprawling stones and forgotten names.

The gold and the painted fascias peel
and in this deserted valley
there is desecration
and among the ruins,
the flattened image and relief,
there are curses.

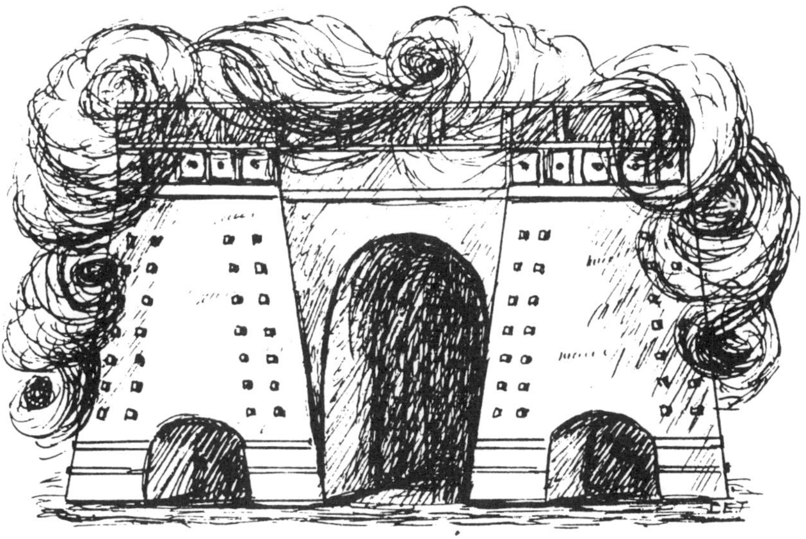

Dowlais Top

The shell
was cast away in a cardboard box,
beached on marl and limestone,
in a car-boot sale on Dowlais Top.

Its smooth underbelly
surfaced from the cheap-jack jetsom
and I heard the song of the sea on Dowlais Top.

In the surge,
wooded peaks and islands
rose from the azure grasp of the Pacific,
where it had slept away the lazy heat of day
among the outstretched coral.

How long had it lain on an arid Dowlais shelf,
while grime barnacled its shell-back?
How long among these rain-lashed hills
of peat and millstone grit?

Did a Dowlais moulder wonder at its form,
or David Jones, Caersalem,
preach of the purity of the water of its Baptism,
or hear in its secret places
a hymn to the sea on Dowlais Top?

Among the wreckage,
half-submerged in the back-wash of depression,
did it withdraw into its slow curve
and listen to the cries of gulls
scavenging on Dowlais Top?

Clydach Ironworks

It is a moonstone in this Fairy Glen,
fired by a Mid-Summer dream
on the bed of Clydach Brook,
and hammered from sleep by Edward Kendall.

Over Smart's Bridge, he drove iron pigs
and down the tramway to Gilwern,
where barges flat-nosed them to Brecon.
A lunatic scheme
in this Fool's Paradise,
without steam or rail or elbow room.

Slag throttled the river,
made it fall and foam on hard-faced rocks
until they flattened.
Bullied them into curves and shapes
until they cracked their faces.

It is a place of skulls.
They mark out spaces in the Council Car Park,
hollow eyes burned out.
A place of fallen giants
whose roots claw at the past
and point to the skeleton of the ironworks.

A place to walk among the buttercups,
accept enchantment from the open-handed trees
and listen to canting water
as it combs the green hair of the river.

Suddenly, the nightmare terrifies,
moth is caught again in the cobweb,
the dereliction, the lack of industry,
and the deja-vue is shattered
by the cries of young lambs.

According to legend, the Fairy Glen, Clydach Ironworks, is the place where Shakespeare wrote 'A Midsummer Night's Dream.'

Manmoel

Old enough,
I climbed Manmoel
to find Dry Docks,
where they told me
ships sailed over the mountain from abroad.

Trees on the edge of the mountain road,
bunched knotted knuckles,
hard as a miners fist,
as if to throw down loaded dice
to the Coal Board game at Marine.

Over the top,
an ocean of wheat rolled
and surged under the hills.
Waves of song poured out
from passengers in Paran chapel,
where old graves lay in ordered rows,
like boats in moorings,
bows facing The Full Moon.

Water welled up at Ton Yr Efail Fach,
and the springs of Pen Rhiw Gyngi
filled the farmers pond at Pen Rhiw Fawddog.

and on Pen-y-Fan Pond
another child sailed a boat.

Gates at Chirk

They hang as iron lace
veiling the red-eyed sky.

In the forging, hammer bruises told,
as elements stretched to breaking point.
Between attachments, chamfered leaves curl
and buds never open.
Tendrils re-coil,
spikes and spears separate
and forked tongues hurt.

Birds, caged in grilles,
cannot stretch their wings to fly,
and songs are welded in their throats.

A family crest dominates,
the faces and the ornamental pieces.
Iron smiles are fixed
and the grimace deepens into pain.
Yet in this solid metal there is humour
and the laughing sun bursts golden in the black.

These gates are locked,
but I shall pass to the lighter side,
where iron transmutes to gold.
Changed to bars
and vibrant strings which harp
on the rhythm in my feet
and the song in my tongue.

To Ruth - Art Student

We loved the sweep and curve of flesh;
the composition, the cool touch of clay,
a white sheet, still life.

We came to Cardiff on the trains
from Rhymney and Ebbw Vale,
and loved the canopies of wooden lace on station buildings,
steamy glass and wet finger faces,
crying through Pontlottyn and Brithdir.

Our common background bound us together
charcoal tips, rows of pastel houses,
downstrokes of chimneys and slant of slates.

We drew Monday baileys
cross-hatched with smalls,
and rag and bone back gardens where Tiger Lillies
cooped behind iron bedsteads,
roared their ginger heads off in the sun.

On our boards,
the scrape of white came through the black,
brought up white colliers in Maclaren's,
their gouged hands clutching at our clumsy cut of light.

One half-term,
there were shadows and spaces between.

I mourned the buried talent.

Ashes

The tip is on fire at Waun-y-pound.
Steel waste
smoulders and fumes stick in the throat.
There is spontaneous combustion,
waste products react on one another
and burst into flame
raging, white-hot.

Molten metal still runs in steelmen's veins,
but their skills are rusting,
they cannot teach their sons
qualities with which they are tempered.
Once resilient and highly tensile,
now they crack under pressure.

On the scrap heap
the fire still rages,
eating into days,
turning them to ash.

Welsh Doll

She is a valued possession,
but her tongue, once fluent
is hidden under a closed mouth.
Her shawl is awry but still pinned around
as defensive as the cloak of Merlin.

The basic thread of her costume has endured
but strained to parting,
although the layers underneath have kept their colour.
The lace, too ripe to touch, softens the severity
of the hard composition of the face.

This Lanover image,
tall hat, white blouse and clean checked apron
is not in my memory.

My hard-wearing grandmother
wore servile flannel,
but on my young skin
it chafed as a hair shirt for my sins
and I threw it off for an English weave of easier material.

Now, I long for the rougher touch
to lick my words into place.

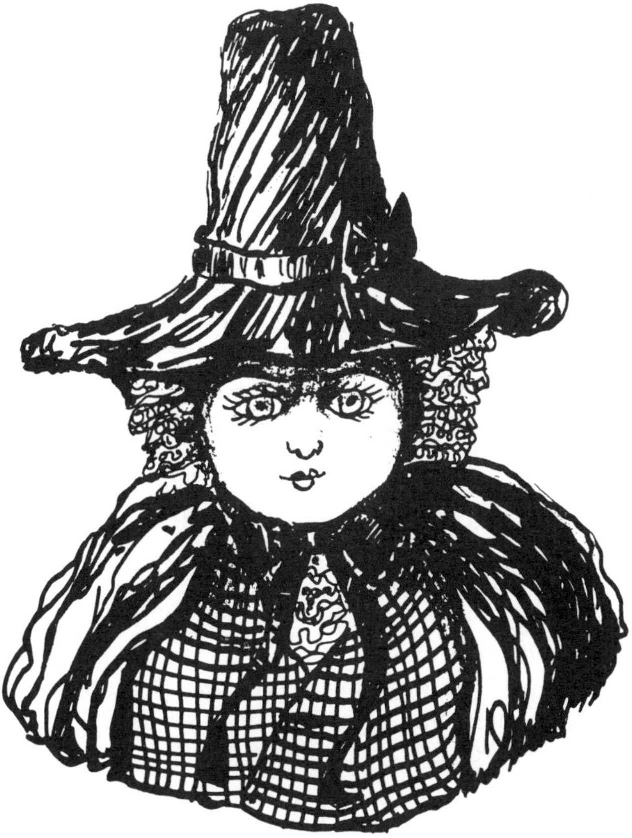

Shadows

Down Cwm,
the sun is shouldered out at half-past-three,
on short shift between the mountains,
Man Moel and Cefn-Yr-Arael,
and Jack is between God and the Devil.

There is no sun in his garden,
kept out by the Wesleyans on one side,
and the beer-bellying walls of the Con. Club
on the other.

He looks down the patched-up sleeve of road
to Marine Colliery,
whose shadow once touched every house.

In that dark tilth, grew the flowers of industry,
and there was bud-burst and no dead-heading.

There were bouquets for bosses,
until a bad smell came under the nose.

Shadows stretch out to cloud the future
and growth is stunted in the shade of unemployment.

Faces are darkened by closure
and fear is in Jack's eyes for his children.
If he keeps hold,
they will wither like cut flowers in his grasp.
Uprooted, they must catch in other soil,
unworked by pick or shovel.

Where the pithead wheel circled the working days,
there is only Bind-weed and Nightshade.
Not a stone stands to cast a shadow,
and in this glare,
there are spectres leaping from the feet of children.

Last Day at Marine Colliery 1991

It is the last day.
The machines are turned off
and breathing is hard
for there is no downcast or upcast of air.
Headgear is torn away
and the wheel no longer churns the river mist,
its broken segments bite the ground.

Steel carrion pulled at outside skins
and jibs tore down the out-buildings,
the Lamp Room, the Baths, and the Washery,
where the face of the coal had a lick and a promise,
in the waters of the Ebbw.

Only the red-bricked stack remains,
a grazed finger, accusing the empty sky.

On this last day,
miners watch from the mountain,
hearts dropping,
as they did when the bond took three minutes to go down.
They remember the butties and the songs,
and the black damp.
Grandfathers, fathers and sons in their turn,
had pride in production
and kept their heads above water.

The last crumbs are scattered for the spirits of the dead
and this explosion is engineered.
Strapped in the belly, the stack buckles,
and bricks course down,
hard tears for lost jobs.

Children skip over grave stones
and search for the iron date,
five pounds a piece,
poor pay for generations.

They cannot put time back, so ask them,
'What will you be when you grow?'
'Don't know, don't know.'

'A policeman', said one,
'and me, and me.'
'What else will you be?'
'Don't know, don't know.'

Their flesh will not carry the deep blue scars
but how will they bear this empty space?

Crying the Rain

When it rains in Cwm,
Manmoel pulls its cap of mohair mist
well down over Spider's Level.

The river bites into the lower lip of the mountain,
and hurls itself against stone gabions,
corseting its sides.
Will, 'More Weather'
shelters in the damp doorway of the Fish Shop,
supping vinegared chips.
Boys waiting their turn,
draw faces on the steamy windows,
and mirror images of names,
are wiped out with weeping.

Housewives,
permed and set from the 'Cut Above'
hurry down the one main street,
dodge drips from acid yellow sale notices,
hanging over-head.

At the end of the road,
where the pit goes down to vanishing point,
the wheel fades in mist and condensation
piping from extractors and ventilators.

Trucks fill up
and roll over blackened sleepers,
to partings,
where women waited in a downpour,
the night of the disaster.

Their cowled flannel shawls
grew heavy on burdened shoulders,
until the fringes cried the rain.

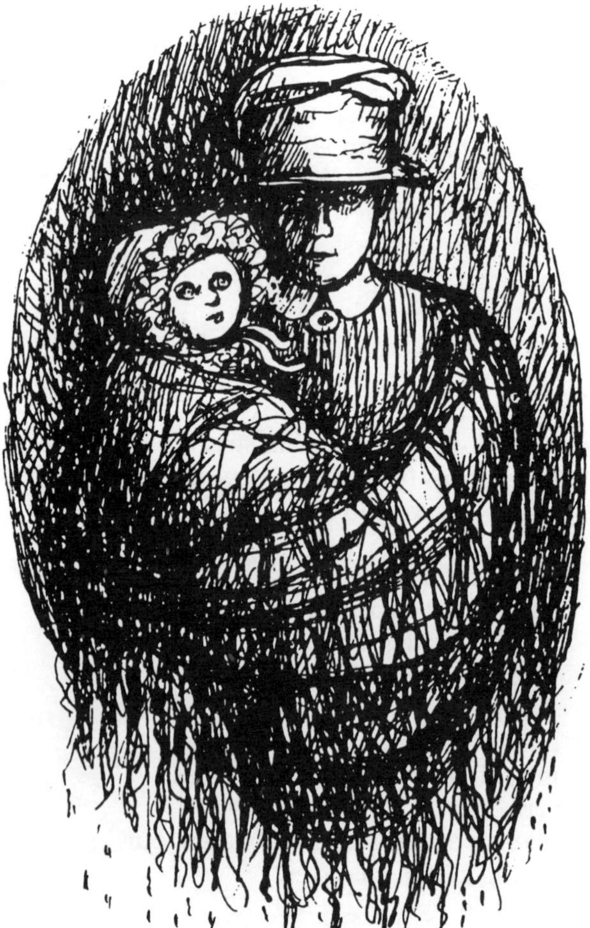

Dead Horse

There's a dead horse in the river at Cwm,
submerged with one dark eye above the surface,
a gaping hole where vultures tear.

White horses in the waters of the Ebbw
buck and race over viscera,
spilled out between Cwm Bridge and Abertillery.

This old work-horse was not Lampos,
a light to shine in dark places,
but Diomedes
eating the flesh of men
gulping them down its throttle,
where black and sweating,
they cut veins deep to feed a body.

They trod over buried bone and hoof,
ate pay-dirt,
between bared teeth and curled lip.
There was some horse-play, and lathering,
and a feed bag at the end of the day.
Then a whiff between whitewashed walls,
with dreams of half-remembered pasture,
and nightmares of thundering drams.

Worked out,
flogging could not revive
and there was no more dragging and wheeling
or pulling between the shafts.

Up top and out of harness,
the broken ribs twist in the carcass
and rot sets in.

We cannot stand the sight
or the stench.

Viewing Platform
Garden Festival 1991

It is a place to watch the alchemy,
the changing of base metal to gold,
to see the selling out and the shortchanging.

In the wind tunnel of Waunlwyd
where the Prince of Wales wiped his dirty boots,
a new carpet is laid between tufts of green,
the unfamiliar shapes and patterns dazzle.

The railway still underlines,
and on embankments young trees sport,
too small for nesting birds, large enough for vultures.

Steam rising from the old work-horse
once clouded vision.
Made of muscle and backbone stiffened with steel,
it filled the valley with muck and money
until nackers moved into Furnace Yard.

Only the flame of Autumn fern and whinberry
recall the burning Bessemer and Open Hearth.
This plastic production will not fire,
it smoulders and fumes stick in the throat.

The surface is glossy and colour hard,
and we need a warmer touch, a feeling for the material.
The oriental silk worm has ousted local sheep
and only a few take bites of new growth
but teeth marks are insignificant.

The blue vinyl lake
is not a true reflection of the grey overhead
and the cascade tumbles like our hopes.

They are building our future in hot-house flowers
and we stand in the cutting wind and shiver.

Stars at the Festival

And the stars came back to earth
for the day
and sang of Welsh heritage,
sighed for nostalgia in newspaper,
fish and chips from the Cwm.

In best B.B.C., they remembered how wonderful it was
when snow was black on the mountain,
running red when it thawed.
Remembered the conical slag,
the sliding down
and how much fun they had.

We stayed
and shovelled the cold from our doorsteps,
trying to keep warm with second-hand promises.
When we reached bottom on ragged behinds,
we wiped smut from our smarting eyes,
and looked for a get-out.

They say we can all sing.
We sang,
for our suppers of Bara-Dwr,
bread and hot water in a cup,
with pepper to give bite.
We had a few tunes,
piping over smash hits
of redundancy and unemployment,
not available on cassette or compact disc.

At the Festival,
they are knocked out at the transformation,
but we only see stars for a twinkling,
and they move away,
out of our orbit.

The Old Story
Garden Festival '92

The story is brought to notice in Welsh and English
in the Garden of Myth and Legend.
The Welsh Dragon fights the pale Saxon beast
who ripped out our mother tongue
and left us speechless in this Eden.

Steam rises,
but in this feeder pond there is no scalding,
only the tight red skin reminds.

A strangled roar from the polystyrene throat
and a wit calles out
'Indigestion'.
It caused a belly-laugh,
but there was burning in the gut.

In this place, we must tell the true story
of the sacrifice and the fatherless boys
not blessed with the cunning of Emrys Wledig.
Our children see the present magic
and leap into the footprints of the beast,
but cannot follow the stamp of boot and nail
embedded underneath.

On the downward path,
the blood of the headless Winifred
wells through stones
and waters of Llangorse wash out treachery.
Around the artificial lake,
ghosts forecast disaster.

The coins of Ifor Bach are banked in earth,
guarded by wing and talon until the men return.
It is an old story,
we have heard it twice before.

Mineral wealth brought Iron Masters
and workers fierce as Twmbarlwm bees
swarmed over mine and furnace.
Then came Bessemer,
and pay-packets bulged with doublers and treblers.

The grip of steel has relaxed,
and men wait with throats cut
and there is no healing
for the wounds are still visible.

Again there is the rush for gold,
and we suffer this Klondyke fever.

In spite of tales we have been told,
we cannot make strides in the Garden,
for worry cripples like Arthur's pebble,
and we cannot hurl it away.

Carousel

Going round in the Festival
you come to the epicentre
and find a circle of horseplay.
The striped canopy is ringed
with a border of laughter-come-to-crying,
white faces plastered with smiles and grimaces
turning cheeks to the chafing wind.

Prancing on barley sugar brass,
the fairground gallopers, jibbers and racers
chase their own tails.
Moulded harness enriched with curlicues,
and names emblazoned on their flanks in scrolls,
catch the eye,
Prince and Wonder, Nib and Dobbin.

Red paint flares in their nostrils
but there is no sensitive area,
they are geared to the raucous music of the organ
and movement is mechanical.

On this money-go-round
the pace is too fast.
We are used to a steady trot like the work-horses
who circled the old granary in stables built on this ground.
Major and Colonel, Sergeant and County.

They felt the crack of the whip
and the bit between clenched teeth,
and were harnessed to haulage
until they had dragged out their days.
At the end, there was no amusement,
their skulls were not dressed with customary ribbon and braid
and there was no masque or music.

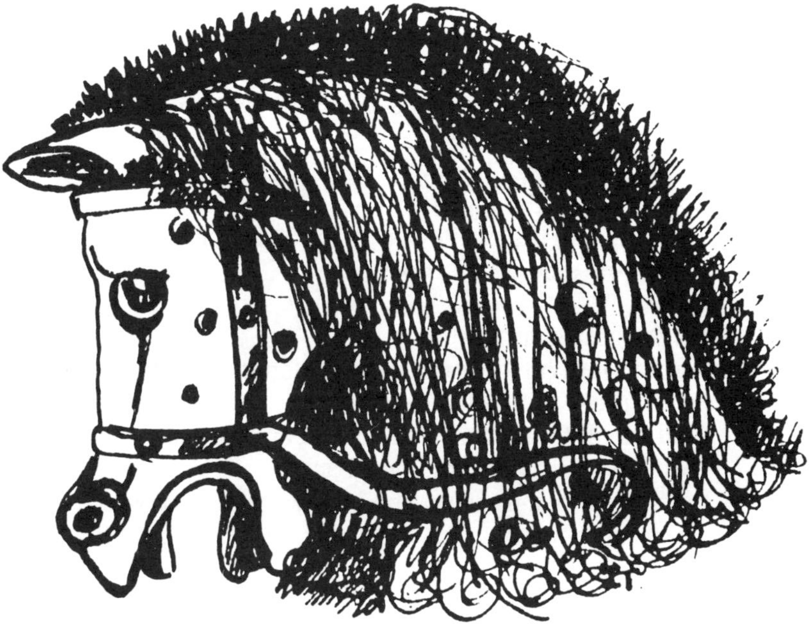

Festival Sweaters

In this rig-out,
the biological white dazzles.
Temperature rises with Festival fever
and there is a rash of shirts
with a slash of red across the chest.

A white heat,
is generated by the fire of Festival,
a Mardi Gras between the dour mountains,
turning their backs on the song and dance.
There is investment in this outfit,
a thicker layer for those who feel the chill,
and underneath a thinner second skin to slip on.
It is part of the exercise,
pulling all ways, 'Ebbw Vale' distorts under excess weight.
Breasts jog under logos,
thrusting like the twin peaks of the Exhibition Hall,
against the side of Manmoel.

On the grey gear,
logos muted on the background, identify the place
where those in need of sweat-shirts
wear the ill-fitting garments of unemployment,
redundancy stamped on their backs.
In this turn-out, they have had the wool pulled over
and remember the cuffs, the sheer neck and the shifts.

In back gardens
limp shadows from the past hang on lines.
Pegged down, the flaccid arms reach out
with no clout to grasp,
or body to resist the buffeting.
In a cooler wash,
white will turn to grey
for the dirt is ingrained.

Young Valley

A geological paper on landslips
told us we were still young.

The mountain masses are moving,
aggravated by natural faults.
Rails twist and buckle and old tracks are useless,
new lines have to be laid down.
Pudding masses move downhill
and ground is unstable.

A sudden movement at Hen Waun
and boulders rolled
through security and family history,
as if called from their Megalithic beds
by Dai the Devil, who had the power.

Among this natural upheaval,
there were diggings,
pits and levels,
their galleries undermining
the stability of stone.

There was a turning over of old ashes for the Festival.
Out-of-the-body wraiths
and moving lights appeared on the mountain.

Spirits haunted conversations
and there was a restlessness, an ancestral fear,
as if the ghosts of Edmund Jones had warned.

Even now,
the ground has not reached the point of natural repose.
The undercurrent is volatile,
but we are young enough to make mistakes.

Gardens

In this Eden,
Methodists, Catholics, Baptists,
the Chorale and the Salvation Army,
sit in the Gods on canvas rainbows
and sing in one ecumenical voice.

In separate denominations
they have wandered in this Garden,
putting their hands together over creation
which took longer than seven days.
They bless the Baptism of the waterfalls
splashing a new name on the forehead of Victoria,
and are thankful for the offering of gardens
from Fisons, the Rotary and Glengettie.

Sculpted in shale,
her hair tangled with vetch and potentilla,
Eve sprawls on the naked mountain,
embracing Man Moel.
The serpentine Cresta snaking at her side,
reminds of forked tongues.

From this eastward garden,
the local Adam has been banished
without one bite of the apple
and looks for sustenance elsewhere.

When praises are over,
the agony begins,
but many have their eyes closed to the kiss.

In the hot-house,
among the spreading hosanna Palms,
the Orchis Maculata, (Gethsemane),
is spattered with red
and succulents have crowns of thorns.

Fossilised

We did not know then
that there were other creatures underfoot,
where the wind still sighed
for company in empty galleries,
where the sea had whispered
and sand softly covered
Spirobis and Estheria,
names foreign to our valley tongue.

They were older than great grandfathers,
rigid in the slow eye of the camera,
holding their breath,
in the strangle-hold of white collars
and the Sunday torture of front and back studs.

Older than great grandmothers,
all buttoned up bosoms, set lips and sepia.

Older than Gran, her hair scraped back to glory,
face crazed with crevices where anger lived.

Older than her potato knife
honed down to a sliver of steel,
slicing like her sharp words through daftness.

Older than our self-important Bible,
begatting under bloated cardboard covers,
holding Moses, Elijah and the Word
in its cold brass clasp.

Memory is imprinted now
with patterns deeply etched,
and in this age, I think
it was a sort of kindness
that we did not know then
what 'old' was.

Cages

On his first day, the wheel turned,
and the world dropped beneath his feet.
At bottom, he was caged in coal,
but the darkness of the headings
receeded in the light of the company he kept
and laughter raised the crushing roof.

After shut-down,
there is no need for early rising
and in the sleep-late mornings,
he watches his lollipop-lady wife,
quarrel with the armholes of her fluorescent mac,
hurrying out to play tic-tac
with school children on the crossing.

In the kitchen,
he picks at his corn-flake breakfast
and silence presses harder than pit walls.
He Fairy's it away, washing dishes
with hands no liquid could soften.

The caged bird pecks at its mirror-image,
'Who's a pretty boy then?'
It turns the wheel underfoot,
and downs a speck of water
like a straight pint.
A strike,
and the bell rings for time out.
It flies to the glass sky in the window,
where the pot-bound Bizzie Lizzie is caught
in net on the never-never.

The bird picks at impacted roots,
a noise from the outside world disturbs
and leaving a bit of luck
on the swank of the Capodimonte ornament,
it goes back to the hanging perch
and the wheel,
where it turns on itself,
worrying until feathers fly.

He angles his small round shaving mirror,
reflecting on closure,
grimaces,
and tries to sing.

Autumn

I hate this burning out,
the final burst of fire.

These trees are overblown
with the confidence of red and yellow,
content with transient beauty,
knowing it will be so again.

Can I be like them,
placid in September warmth,
knowing that after sleep will come green fire
and I will stand in it like Ayesha,
renewed until the flame turns red.

Somewhere, before the end of summer,
the green no longer surges
and the life force drops.
The withering was not there yesterday,
but now crow's feet are visible as bloom fades.
Cold winds comb through
and the thinning chestnut falls.
What do I care
for palliatives of wisdom and experience?
The brown leaf of Autumn mottles my skin
and the tracery of veins stand out.
Each Autumn, they shed their yearly burden
and few are felled by storms because of weight.
They know release, the weightlessness
as tears fall in yellow pools around their feet.

Children catch falling colours and bear them up,
but in this long season the burden grows heavy
and there are no children.

Is there then only this season,
or after winter,
will there be another ring to mark the growth,
another gleam of gold?

Crying China Man

His face was aged to yellow ochre
and cracked, but without laughter lines.
A breath could part the warp and weft
of his saffron robe
and in the slim, dark, doll eyes,
there was no white to brighten.
Blinds drawn to black out the hollow
carved by a child's death.

He lay in a narrow drawer,
without ears to listen to a century go by,
from Iron Master to Iron Lady,
he was untouched,
as if another child's hand would sully memory.

He came from another culture
of embroidered silks and ceremonial tea,
to a place with a shared interest in dragons,
but where women had a broader tread
bound up with working boots.

Under a layer of tissue,
his cry was in his belly
for some sorrows are not meant for sleeves.

There are those who cry 'Mama' with ill-usage,
up-ended and breath knocked out,
but he needed the right touch.

I held him in my hand,
not knowing then it had been forbidden,
and under pressure,
pent up for a hundred years,
he cried.

Epitaph

It is an effort to get there
so high up, you expect to see the angel at the gate.

It is a place to catch breath,
this burial ground,
where the wind gives stinging back-handers
and tears are snatched away in the eye of the wind.

I slot Irises in the holes provided
and the mauve petals
swing away from the cold touch of marble
as if the name of 'Edwin Aaron' could hurt.

In this soil
are we no more than daisies,
opening our faces to the day to mirror the sun,
as newly bright as
the gold-leaf letters 'Ida Kate',
deeply cut.

It cannot end here in this wild place,
disciplined only by uniform headstones
and the regulation six feet.

Here, the cobwebs of dreams are blown from the senses
and the emptiness hurts,
letting in other devils,
that even God has no answer for.

I know it is faithless to cling to stone,
but I need the material,
a place to come and weep.